Original title:
Wild Love

Copyright © 2024 Book Fairy Publishing
All rights reserved.

Editor: Theodor Taimla
Author: Isabella Ilves
ISBN HARDBACK: 978-9916-756-50-8
ISBN PAPERBACK: 978-9916-756-51-5

Windswept Lovers

Beneath the sky, a love so true
Where winds caress the morning dew
They whisper tales of hearts aligned
In breezes soft, their fate entwined

Upon the cliffs, where seagulls cry
Two souls embrace, eternally
Their love a force, both wild and free
Like winds that dance across the sea

In moonlit nights, they find their grace
Two spirits lost in time and space
A gust that binds their hearts forever
Windswept lovers, parting never

Earthbound Affection

Underneath the ancient oak
Their hearts did intertwine and spoke
Of love both soft and deeply planted
In soil rich, their wishes granted

Through seasons' change, their bond remains
In sunshine bright or falling rains
Earth holds their story close and dear
A testament, enduring here

With every root and leaf they share
A lifetimes' worth of tender care
Together in the firm embrace
Of earthbound love, they find their place

Feral Devotion

In moonlit glade where wild hearts beat
Untamed desire, shadows fleet
Whispers of night, fierce love ignites
Through tangled boughs, relentless flights

Claws of longing, we rend the skies
With primal yowls, no dark disguise
Together strong, our spirits steel
Feral devotion, wounds will heal

Eyes gleaming bright, through forest thick
With every step, our pulses quick
Roots intertwine beneath our feet
In nature's cradle, love replete

Ecstatic Mania

In chaos born, we dance the flame
Spirits wild, none can tame
Mind unbound, thoughts collide
Ecstatic mania, no place to hide

Sky ablaze with frantic dreams
We soar as one, or so it seems
Pulse electric, nerves aflame
In this tempest, none to blame

Embrace the storm, let madness twirl
Hearts entwined, a fevered swirl
Reality, a fragile thread
In mania's grip, we are led

Unconventional Romance

No roses red nor candles bright
In cryptic codes, our love alight
Anomalies in crowded halls
Whisper secrets through the walls

Against the grain, our path we tread
Uncharted realms where few dare to tread
In every glance, an art defined
Unconventional hearts intertwined

No need for norms, we forge our way
Moments stolen from the fray
In whispers soft, in hidden glance
We thrive in our defiant dance

Primitive Yearning

Beneath the stars, the ancient call
Echoes of time, we heed them all
Fire in the blood, a primal thrum
To earth's raw heart, we succumb

In caves deep, our roots extend
To origins where souls transcend
Desire raw, unshaped by fear
In every pulse, old gods revere

Voices past and future blend
Yearning primal, never to end
Through wood and stone, by wild fire
Primitive love, our fierce conspire

Infatuation's Edge

Upon the edge of longing, I stand
Lost in a fervor I can't withstand
Your gaze, a magnet pulling me through
An infatuation, both old and new

Heartbeats echo in the silence of night
Whispers of dreams, just out of sight
The moonlight dances on your face
In your presence, time finds no pace

Every word you say, a song to my ear
Drowning doubts, quelling fear
On the precipice of love's embrace
In your eyes, I find my place

Senseless Charm

A charm unspoken, a silent allure
Feelings so strong, yet so demure
Your smile, a beacon in the dark
Ignites in me, a fervent spark

Soft touches, your hand in mine
Universes converge, stars align
No need for words, nor grand display
In your presence, I lose my way

Eyes that speak of endless dreams
Moments stolen, eternal it seems
The world fades to a mere hum
By your senseless charm, I am undone

Unrestrained Temptation

Temptation's call, a siren's song
In your embrace, I belong
Bound by desire, wild and free
In your touch, I find the key

Unchained, our passions ignite
A dance of shadows in the night
No boundaries, no lines to draw
In your love, I find my law

The taste of you, a sweet delight
A story written in the night
Unrestrained, our hearts collide
Together, no secrets to hide

Wilderness Kisses

In the wilderness, we find our bliss
Nature's kiss, an untamed twist
Beneath the canopy of green so high
Our love ascends, touching the sky

Soft whispers of the forest breeze
In your arms, time seems to freeze
Birds sing songs of endless love
Our vows, blessed by skies above

Feet on earth, hearts in flight
We embrace the wilderness of night
Kisses shared, wild and profound
In nature's arms, we are unbound

Wildfire Hearts

Beneath the crimson, twilight skies,
Our love ignites where wild winds rise,
Flames that dance in fervent art,
We burn as one, wild in heart.

Ember whispers, secrets tell,
In your gaze, a charming spell,
Boundless passion, never part,
We are echoes of the heart.

In the woods where shadows creep,
Love's inferno, vast and deep,
Silent vows and fervent starts,
Forever blaze, wildfire hearts.

Savage Symphony

In the night's untamed embrace,
Music wild, no gentle trace,
Notes that roar and voices free,
Our love's savage symphony.

Thunderous drums, a rhythm fierce,
Harmony that shadows pierce,
On the stage where wild things be,
We compose our symphony.

Two hearts clash in vibrant song,
Echoes pure, both weak and strong,
In the storm, our spirits flee,
Lost in savage symphony.

Exotic Passion

In a land where dreams are spun,
Underneath a foreign sun,
Eyes that promise, lips that fashion,
Worlds entwine in exotic passion.

Perfumed nights and silken skies,
Whispered secrets, tender sighs,
Hands explore where hearts can ration,
Every touch an exotic passion.

Wild gardens, untamed streams,
Love that flows in mystic dreams,
In this fervent, lush contraption,
We are bound by exotic passion.

Unrestrained Allure

In the dance of moonlit night,
Beauty raw and pure delight,
Eyes that gleam through shadows pure,
Lost within your unrestrained allure.

Silken strands that winds caress,
Whispers soft, a lover's guess,
Nature's song, a sweet detour,
Led astray by unrestrained allure.

Stars above, a witness sent,
To the love by fate's consent,
Bound in charm, we can't ignore,
Falling for your unrestrained allure.

Exotic Affection

In lands where sun and shadows play,
A love unique, both wild and tame.
Your touch, a breeze, the night at bay,
Exotic whispers call my name.

Our hearts entwine in secret tunes,
Beyond the reach of worldly bounds.
By moonlit pools and afternoons,
We find our place, where peace surrounds.

In labyrinths of ancient art,
With colors rare and stories deep,
We cherish every beat, each part,
In memories vivid, a love we keep.

Fierce Bonds

Through tempests wild, our spirits meld,
Unbroken ties in stormy seas.
Our strength within, a force withheld,
A bond that brings the world to knees.

In battles fierce, with swords aflame,
We stand as one, unwaveringly.
Against the winds, we stake our claim,
Together strong, and fierce, and free.

When shadows fall, and doubts do creep,
We face the dark, undaunted still.
For in each other, vows we keep,
A bond no time, nor test, can kill.

Wilderness of Passion

Beneath the sky where eagles soar,
Our hearts beat wild, untamed and free.
In nature's arms, we seek and more,
A wilderness of passion's plea.

Among the pines, with whispers hushed,
We find each other, raw and true.
In shadows deep, desires flushed,
A world reborn in vibrant hue.

With every kiss, an ancient fire,
In wilderness, our spirits merge.
Endless love, our only choir,
On passion's timeless, sacred verge.

Liberation of Lust

In twilight's grasp, our yearnings freed,
A dance of shadows, bold and bright.
In every touch, a fervent need,
We burn like stars, defy the night.

Our bodies speak in whispered tones,
A symphony of urgent cries.
No chains withstand our heated moans,
We rise as one, unite the skies.

In clandestine embrace, we soar,
No boundaries hold our fervid quest.
In liberation, we implore,
A lust fulfilled, our souls at rest.

Rapture in Rebellion

In whispering winds of daring might,
Hearts unchained take trembling flight,
Against the shadows, shadows fall,
Rebels rise at freedom's call.

Echoes of a sacred flame,
Through silent night, they shape the same,
A world re-forged in gleaming light,
Emerges bold from endless night.

Fingerprints on dreams uncast,
Vows to break the fettered past,
Unyielding spirits sing the fight,
A rapture found in darkest night.

Through shattered glass and iron bars,
They seek their fate among the stars,
In steadfast hearts, rebellion grows,
A courage only freedom knows.

Boundless tides in stormy seas,
A raptured spirit whispers free,
With every pulse, a vision forms,
The dawn reborn in raging storms.

Savage Intensity

Underneath a blood-red sky,
Wolves of fortune prowl and cry,
Intensity in every beat,
Savage hearts that know no fleet.

Raw as earth and fierce as flame,
They roam through life without a name,
Vivid dreams and sharpened eyes,
Chase the echoes of their cries.

Veins of steel and nerves of ice,
Carry burdens, pay the price,
Passions wild, untamed and free,
Fuel the fire of destiny.

To the edges of despair,
Savage spirits face the dare,
Naked truths in shadows cast,
Walk the lines of future past.

Relentless and unbowed they stride,
Through the tempest, side by side,
In every scar, a tale they spell,
Of savage lives they dared to tell.

Elusive Eternity

In shadows' dance where whispers play,
Eternal moments slip away,
Fleeting echoes, morning rays,
Chasing dreams in twilight's gaze.

Time's embrace a tender theft,
Leaving souls in silence left,
Glimpses of forever's breath,
Lost in labyrinths of depth.

Stars etch secrets, cosmos' art,
Winds of fate that worlds impart,
Infinite yet fragile start,
Bound within a fragile heart.

Reflections in a mirrored sea,
Rippled paths in mystery,
Ephemeral our destiny,
Seeking what cannot yet be.

Through veils of night, we softly tread,
Eternal yearnings softly spread,
In endless awe where dreams are led,
Elusive echoes overhead.

Ferocious Zeal

Burning bright with untamed fire,
Driven by a fierce desire,
Passion's flame ascends much higher,
In hearts that fiercely never tire.

Through the storm and through the rain,
Zeal unbridled, breaking chains,
Resilience running through their veins,
Defying odds, embracing pain.

Eyes ablaze with dreams confined,
Strength of will and iron mind,
No boundary that can bind,
Their spirit's force, unaligned.

Conquering mountains, roaring seas,
Undeterred by gentle pleas,
A force of nature, meant to seize,
The challenges on bended knees.

Relentless drive, undaunted soul,
With every step, achieving goals,
Ferocious zeal that makes us whole,
An unstoppable, burning scroll.

Eccentric Romance

In a world of quirky dreams,
Love unravels at the seams,
Dances wild in moonlight beams,
Eccentric hearts, where passion streams.

Candles flicker, shadows play,
Laughing through the night and day,
Rhythms in a kaleidoscope display,
Unpredictable, in love's ballet.

Magic spun with silken threads,
Tales of whimsy, softly spread,
Adventures in the paths they tread,
Bound by hearts uniquely wed.

Whispered secrets, stolen glance,
Twilight's glow in sweet romance,
In their odd, enchanting trance,
Lovers twirl in fate's sweet dance.

Through the layers of the night,
Love's embrace a vibrant light,
Eccentric paths, forever bright,
In each other's arms, delight.

Raging Hearts

In the tempest of desire,
Hearts ablaze with fierce fire,
Passions soar and never tire,
Bound by love's consuming pyre.

Eyes meet, souls collide,
In this storm, there's no divide,
Riding waves of passion's tide,
Forever united side by side.

Thunder rolls and lightning bright,
In their love, a wild flight,
Raging hearts in darkest night,
Together, they ignite the sky.

Torrents of emotion rise,
Echoes of their fervent cries,
Finding truth in lover's eyes,
In each other's arms, they lie.

In this storm where hearts entwine,
Bound by love, a force divine,
Raging hearts in endless line,
Eternal flames that brightly shine.

Forbidden Forest

Whispers of the ancient trees
Secrets buried in the leaves
Silent paths where shadows creep
Mysteries the woods do keep

In the twilight, spirits soar
Guardians of lore old and sore
Roots entwined like fate's own thread
Where the brave and curious tread

Moonlight glistens on the brook
Pages of a darkened book
Echoes of forgotten strife
Breathing echoes back to life

Fern and vine in shadows play
Keeping light of dawn at bay
Concealed within this verdant sea
Lies the forest's hidden plea

Tread with caution, wanderer
In the haunts of arboreal ker
For once you're in this wooded glade
You may dream but not evade

Untamed Zephyr

Breezes whisper through the pines
Songs of far-off, distant climes
Dance of leaves in wild embrace
Airborne in an endless chase

Mountains bow to restless air
Carrying with it scents so rare
Free, unbounded, wild and new
Gales that sing the sky so blue

Ever-moving, never still
Chasing down the wind's own will
Zephyr's kiss on parched dry land
Lending life with gentle hand

Whispered secrets, quiet force
Changing paths in endless course
Skyward freedom's untamed friend
Journey's start, without an end

Feel the touch, the wild breeze
Promise woven through the trees
In its arms lies grace unseen
In its breath, the world's serene

Restless Hearts

Midnight musings, troubled dreams
Love beneath the starry beams
Yearnings echo in the night
Silent prayers in moon's soft light

Hearts that wander, never rest
Questing for what seems the best
In the darkness, hopes aloft
Seeking places warm and soft

Distance cannot still their beat
Longing eyes, they search, they meet
Through the veils of sleepless hours
Plucking dreams like fragrant flowers

Shadows cast by hearts that ache
Bound by whispers they can't shake
In the quiet, love takes flight
Restless souls throughout the night

Morning light brings weary eyes
Yet the heart, it never lies
For within its steady beat
Love and longing always meet

Wolves in Love

Beneath the moon's ethereal glow
Two wolves in love, hearts aflow
Their howls a chorus, wild and free
Bonded by an ancient decree

In the forest deep and wide
Together they in shadows hide
Silver fur and golden eyes
Reflecting stars in midnight skies

Paws that tread on dew-kissed ground
Silently, where love is found
Echoes of their union strong
Weaving through the night a song

Hunger not for flesh nor fight
But for kinship in the night
In each breath, a tender nudge
In each step, their hearts adjudge

Moon above, their witness true
As they vow forever to
In the wild, their souls align
Wolves in love, their hearts entwine

Unbridled Affection

Beyond the dawn where shadows fade,
Two hearts in twilight serenade,
Love's whispers in the quiet night,
A bond unbroken, pure delight.

In starlit skies, our souls align,
Through valleys deep, oaths intertwined,
Your touch, a balm to needless fears,
We dance through boundless, timeless years.

No chains can bind this fervent grace,
A tender kiss, your warm embrace,
Together, ever we shall roam,
In each other's hearts, our home.

Through storms that rage and skies ablaze,
With strength that cherished love conveys,
Forever, darling, side by side,
In passion's tide, our hearts confide.

Unbridled is our glowing flame,
Love's joyous hymn we dare proclaim,
For in your gaze, my truest friend,
A love eternal till the end.

Raw Affinity

In whispered winds, your name I chant,
Through fields of dreams, our spirits grant,
A serenade of wild embrace,
Two souls enkindled, face to face.

In moonlit paths where shadows play,
Our hearts converge, no words to say,
A touch, a glance, an endless flight,
Together soaring through the night.

No chains to bind, no fears to hide,
In raw affinity, we bide,
An essence pure, a fervor wild,
Within your eyes, I find the child.

We carve our tales in silent guise,
Through whispered breaths and longing sighs,
Each moment shared, a gift of fate,
In passion's realm, we navigate.

A love unbound by space or time,
In perfect harmony, we rhyme,
For in your heart, my soul finds rest,
Together, ever, blessed.

Primal Desire

In shadows deep, where silence speaks,
A fervent pulse, our passion seeks,
Untamed, unbridled, fierce and free,
Your touch, the fire, ignites in me.

Eyes that burn with molten flame,
In whispered vows, we cast no shame,
Desire's dance, a wild spree,
Two hearts that beat in raw decree.

Through midnight's veil, our secrets wove,
In primal charge, we dare to rove,
A kiss, a breath, a silken snare,
Together lost without a care.

No words can tame this wild affair,
In heated night, we boldly dare,
Desire's path, our chosen flight,
We burn as one through endless night.

In primal tides, our spirits meld,
No chains, no bounds, no truths withheld,
For in your arms, my soul's delight,
In primal love, we find our light.

Untethered Souls

In fields where daylight softly springs,
Our spirits soar on whisperings,
Untethered, free, on wings of flight,
Together through the endless night.

A journey charted by the heart,
Where dreams and reality impart,
In every step, a promise told,
Our love, a story to unfold.

No chains to bind, no walls confine,
In sacred bond, our hearts align,
Untethered, wild, our spirits blend,
Through every storm, we transcend.

In twilight's glow, we find our way,
Through darkness, into light of day,
With hands entwined and love's embrace,
In each other's eyes, our solace.

Through boundless realms, our love shall soar,
A timeless dance, forevermore,
For in your love, my soul knows peace,
Untethered, whole, our joys increase.

Primal Attraction

In twilight's hush, our gazes meet,
Where hearts align, a rhythm's beat.
Desires spark, like stars above,
In primal dance, two souls in love.

Your touch ignites, a fierce embrace,
In shadows deep, we find our place.
Words unspoken, silence speaks,
A longing flame, that passion seeks.

Eyes convey what lips conceal,
A yearning tide we cannot steal.
Tangled limbs, a fevered chase,
In twilight's fold, we leave no trace.

Magnetized by scent and sigh,
In primal urge, together lie.
Bound by forces, raw and true,
In rapture's grip, we are renewed.

From dusk till dawn, the night unfolds,
In primal call, a love extols.
With every breath, a bond so tight,
Entwined as one, till morning's light.

Enthralling Worlds

Beyond the veil, where dreams reside,
In lands unseen, our spirits glide.
Enthralled by visions, vast and free,
In boundless realms of reverie.

Mountains whisper, rivers sing,
In every turn, enchantments bring.
Forgotten paths, where wonders lay,
In secret worlds, we lose the day.

Stars like beacons, guide our flight,
Through timeless skies of endless night.
Mystic forests, oceans wide,
In every heart, enchantments hide.

Creatures wondrous, tales untold,
In entrancing worlds, adventures bold.
With each step, a magic found,
In endless dreams where we are bound.

In these realms, our souls take wing,
To music only we can sing.
Enthralled by worlds both near and far,
In dreamy lands, where we are stars.

Forbidden Flames

In shadowed alcoves, whispers low,
Where secret fires softly glow.
Forbidden love, a hidden spark,
In darkest night, ignites the dark.

A touch that sears, a stolen glance,
In passion's grip, we dare to dance.
Behind closed doors, a secret kept,
In silken dreams where lovers slept.

The world outside, a distant roar,
In whispered vows, we seek no more.
Entwined in shadows, hearts aflame,
In secret trysts, we play the game.

Waves of heat, in silent rush,
Our love concealed in twilight hush.
In hidden places, we confess,
The forbidden flame we both possess.

Though fate may cast a shadowed veil,
Our secret love shall not grow pale.
In clandestine fire, we remain,
In hidden worlds where hearts unchain.

Untrammeled Bliss

In fields of gold, where freedoms sigh,
Our spirits soar, we touch the sky.
Untrammeled bliss, a boundless sea,
In open arms, we breathe so free.

No chains to bind, no walls confine,
In endless joy, our hearts align.
With every step, the world unfolds,
In boundless love, our story holds.

We dance through meadows, wild and fair,
In untrammeled bliss, without a care.
The breeze our song, the stars our guide,
In love's embrace, we gently glide.

Mountains call with echoes clear,
In endless paths, we wander near.
With every kiss, our spirits rise,
In unchained love, devoid of ties.

In this vast expanse of heart and mind,
We find the world, no bounds confined.
Untrammeled bliss we now possess,
In timeless love, we are our best.

Fiery Eden

Amid the embers, fate takes flight,
Blazing trails in the dead of night,
Whispers of warmth, a golden dawn,
In this garden of fire, we are reborn.

Fragrant heat and glowing leaves,
A dance of flames, where heart believes,
Passions flare, igniting dreams,
In a realm where love redeems.

By molten rivers, shadows play,
Light and dark in grand display,
Tender touch of burning kiss,
In a paradise ablaze with bliss.

Stars align in fiery arcs,
Guiding souls through endless sparks,
A symphony of heat and light,
Eden's flames, an eternal night.

In the inferno, hearts embrace,
Finding solace in the blaze,
For in the warmth of love's inferno,
Eden's fire shall forever glow.

Wilderness Whisper

In the hush of forest deep,
Nature's secrets softly keep,
Winds that murmur through the pines,
Echoes of forgotten lines.

Beneath the canopy so grand,
Whispers weave through timeless land,
Leaves that rustle, streams that sigh,
Wild heartbeats, earth and sky.

Shadows dance in dappled light,
Silent songs of ancient night,
Through the wild, a voice calls,
Wilderness within us all.

Mountains, valleys, sacred ground,
In the silence, truth is found,
Dreams take flight on feathered wings,
In the whisper, nature sings.

Boundless beauty, life's embrace,
In the wild, we find our place,
Lost in echoes, found anew,
Wilderness will guide us through.

Elemental Amour

Waves that kiss the sandy shore,
Elemental love, forevermore,
Columns of wind in gentle sway,
Breath of amore, lead the way.

Fire's warmth in evening's glow,
Passion's heartstrings start to show,
Earth's embrace of rooted ground,
Love eternal, deeply bound.

Lightning dances through the storm,
Lover's pulse in purest form,
Raindrops fall, a tender touch,
Nature's symphony, saying much.

Stars alight in velvet sky,
Promises of love on high,
Unified through cosmic chords,
Infinite, our hearts' accords.

In the balance of the earth,
Find the love, restore its worth,
Elemental, strong and free,
Bound in purest unity.

Forest of Affection

Under ancient oak's embrace,
Hearts entwined in sacred space,
Leaves that whisper soft and true,
In the forest, love renew.

Paths that wind through verdant green,
Love's own secret, unseen,
In the shadows, light does play,
Guiding us along the way.

Roots are deep, like bonds we share,
Growing stronger through the care,
Each new bud, affection's bloom,
In this forest, we find room.

Canopy of stars above,
Sheltering our endless love,
Whispers float on evening breeze,
Promising eternal ease.

In this woodland, hearts align,
Nature sings a love divine,
Forest deep, with love entwined,
Forever yours, forever mine.

Passionate Outburst

Fires ignite in the depths of my soul,
Burning wild, beyond my control.
Whispers of fervor, strong and clear,
Louder than doubt, stronger than fear.

A tempest roars in my quickening heart,
Each beat echoes a thunderous start.
Emotions surge, crest, and flow,
A torrent of passion begins to show.

Desire flames in a desperate plea,
Yearning for all that I can be.
In this outburst, I find my place,
Amidst the chaos, a fleeting grace.

Unrestrained, I kiss the sky,
On wings of love, I soar and fly.
Consumed by fire, pure and true,
In this passionate outburst, I renew.

Savage Tenderness

In the wildness of a tender gaze,
A feral love sets hearts ablaze.
A dance of rage, yet soft and mild,
In savage tenderness, we are beguiled.

Claws of compassion scratch the soul,
Digging tenderly, making us whole.
With ferocity and gentle might,
We navigate the day and night.

A storm of feelings, fierce embrace,
In the wilderness, we find our place.
Wildflowers bloom in shadows cast,
Where savage tenderness will forever last.

In love's rough and gentle light,
We find solace in the fight.
Hand in hand, as one we stand,
Savage tenderness, our sacred land.

Beastly Beauty

In the eyes of a beast, I find,
A beauty wild, untamed, unkind.
Hidden grace in every flaw,
A fierce allure, a voiceless call.

Strength and power, raw and free,
A savage beauty, wild like the sea.
Untamable, yet pure and true,
In every glance, a world anew.

Amidst the fangs and claws that gleam,
Lies a heart of a silenced dream.
A beast unmasked, yet beauty stays,
In primal nights and twilight days.

Nature's art, both wild and sweet,
In beastly beauty, we find our beat.
An untamed dance, a harmony,
Intricate, fierce, forever free.

Rapturous Wilderness

Among the trees, in verdant glow,
A rapturous wilderness, wild and slow.
Whispers of leaves, the song of streams,
In nature's embrace, we live our dreams.

Under the canopy, stars ignite,
A dance of shadows, pure delight.
In moonlit meadows, we find our grace,
The wilderness, our sacred place.

Mountains rise to kiss the sky,
Echoing calls of birds that fly.
In this rapture, we breathe and grow,
Untamed beauty, a natural flow.

Through forest trails and winding ways,
We lose ourselves in endless days.
In the wild, our spirits find,
A rapturous peace, of heart and mind.

Jungle Fever

In the heart of emerald green,
Where sunlight filters through the leaves,
A world unknown, a dream unseen,
Where nature whispers and deceives.

Monkeys swing from tree to tree,
Their calls a symphony in the air,
A dance of life, wild and free,
In this jungle, pure and rare.

Tigers prowl with eyes that gleam,
Silent shadows in the night,
The jungle's pulse a constant theme,
In the moon's silver light.

The river flows, a winding vein,
Reflecting skies of golden hue,
The jungle's beauty, wild and plain,
Ever ancient, ever new.

In the depths, where few may roam,
Mysteries and secrets lie,
The jungle's fever is its home,
Beneath the vast and endless sky.

Thunderous Adoration

Clouds converge in twilight hues,
A storm brews in whispers low,
Nature's passion, wild and loose,
In the winds that fiercely blow.

Lightning splits the brooding sky,
A lover's touch, electric fire,
In the thunder's rolling cry,
Echoes of profound desire.

Rain falls down in silver streams,
Kissing earth with tender grace,
In every drop, a lover's dreams,
In each caress, a warm embrace.

Thunder roars, a beast unleashed,
Announcing love in mighty tone,
In the tempest, hearts find peace,
In the storm, they're not alone.

As the tempest finds its rest,
And calm returns to evening's glow,
Thunderous adoration, blessed,
In nature's fervor, love does grow.

Beastly Emotions

In the forest, deep and dark,
Where shadows flit and roam,
Lies a place with beastly mark,
A wild, untamed home.

Wolves howl under moonlit skies,
Their calls a haunting song,
In their eyes, emotions rise,
Piercing, fierce, and strong.

Bears roam wide in solitude,
In forests dense and deep,
Beastly hearts with thoughts imbued,
Guarding secrets they keep.

Eagles soar on wings of might,
Majestic, bold, and free,
Beastly spirits in their flight,
Of raw intensity.

In the wild where beasts reside,
Emotions thrive unbound,
In their eyes, the tides confide,
A world profound, profound.

Elemental Passion

Fire dances, wild and bright,
A lover's flame, intense and pure,
In the night, it takes its flight,
An ember's passion to endure.

Water whispers, soft and sweet,
A flowing touch, so cool and deep,
Elemental hearts that beat,
In waves of dreams, they sleep.

Earth stands firm, strong and true,
A foundation vast and grand,
Elemental strength we knew,
In every grain of ancient sand.

Wind caresses with a sigh,
A breath of love, so free and warm,
Elemental, bold and spry,
In every gust, a heart takes form.

In the blend of earth and sky,
Where elements do intertwine,
Passion's spirit cannot lie,
In every essence, love does shine.

Chaos in Ecstasy

Whirlwind whispers in the night,
Moonlit shadows, silver bright.
Stars cascade like falling dreams,
In the chaos, love redeems.

Passion's flame ignites the air,
Hearts entwine, beyond compare.
Ecstasy within our reach,
Silent screams, a wordless speech.

Hands that wander, craving more,
Boundless fervor, spirits soar.
Entangled souls, we lose control,
In the chaos, we are whole.

Time dissolves, no seconds trace,
Loving madness, pure embrace.
Whispers turn to symphonies,
In the chaos, harmony.

Tangled fates, a dance so wild,
Chaos births a love beguiled.
In this fevered, frenzied plea,
Chaos breathes our ecstasy.

Feral Delirium

Wild hearts in the boundless dark,
Eyes that blaze with a primal spark.
Nature calls in moonlit cries,
In feral dreams, our spirit flies.

Untamed whispers, wild and free,
In the night, our destiny.
Roaming paths where shadows creep,
In delirium, secrets keep.

Wolves that howl, a hidden tune,
Stars dance round a scarlet moon.
Passions, fierce, no chains confine,
In feral love, souls entwine.

Forest deep, a sacred ground,
Rhythms beat, a timeless sound.
In our flesh, the wild's decree,
In delirium, spirits flee.

Nocturnal rites, our hearts unbind,
Feral dreams, no fear of mind.
In this tempest, raw and true,
We embrace the wild in you.

Primitive Pining

Hearts that ache with ancient call,
Love unmoved by rise and fall.
Primal whispers in the air,
Primitive in pining's snare.

In the forest's deep embrace,
Eyes that search, a lover's trace.
Echoes from a bygone time,
Yearning in a wordless rhyme.

Hands that touch with timeless grace,
Fingers lost in warm embrace.
Pining for a love so vast,
Tied to a primordial past.

Nature speaks in leaf and breeze,
Songs of longing in the trees.
Primitive in every sigh,
Underneath a boundless sky.

Ancient runes in hearts unfold,
Stories of a love untold.
In the pining, old as stone,
Primitive, we find our own.

Raucous Heartbeats

Thunder in the silent night,
Hearts that race with wild delight.
Drums of passion, clash and call,
Raucous heartbeats, one and all.

Eyes that meet with fierce desire,
Burning like a raging fire.
In the whirlwind, souls converge,
Heartbeats ride a common surge.

Skin that hums with electric touch,
Craving, needing, wanting much.
In the chaos, love's sweet thrill,
Raucous heartbeats, never still.

Breathless whispers, echoed cries,
In this fervor, no disguise.
Pounding rhythms, wild and loud,
Heartbeats lost within the crowd.

Harmony in the storm we dance,
Living in a frenzied trance.
In the raucous, we shall find,
Heartbeats beating, love entwined.

Relentless Yearning

In dreams, I traverse distant lands,
Where whispers of the heart expand,
A restless soul, forever seeks,
The truth beyond what silence speaks.

Stars that fall, ignite the night,
Casting shadows in soft light,
A journey bound by hope's embrace,
Relentless yearning in the chase.

Oceans vast and mountains tall,
I wander through them all,
For in the wind, your voice I hear,
A love profound, yet ever near.

Through deserts dry and forests deep,
Where secrets long forgotten sleep,
My heart persists, defies the end,
In search of you, my dearest friend.

The twilight's glow, the dawn's first hue,
Each moment brings me close to you,
Relentless yearning fuels my stride,
Till fate unites us side by side.

Nature's Lovers

Underneath the whispering trees,
We find our love in quiet ease,
The rustle of leaves, the birds' sweet song,
In nature's arms, we both belong.

The river's flow, the mountains grand,
We walk together, hand in hand,
Each step we take, a bond renews,
In every dawn, our love ensues.

The meadow blooms in colors bright,
The stars awaken with the night,
Beside the fire, in its warm glow,
Nature's love begins to show.

Through changing seasons, summer's heat,
Winter's cold, or autumn's greet,
Our love, like roots of ancient trees,
Grows deeper through the gentle breeze.

Beneath the sky, vast and clear,
We hold each other ever near,
In nature's lovers, joy we've found,
In harmony, our hearts are bound.

Untamed Bond

In fields where wildflowers sway,
Our untamed bond finds its way,
No chains to hold, no walls confine,
A love that's purely yours and mine.

Beneath the sun's unyielding blaze,
We dance in freedom's glowing haze,
A spirit wild, a heart so free,
In nature's grip, we choose to be.

Through stormy nights and winds that wail,
Our unwavering hearts prevail,
No tempest fierce can break the mold,
Of love that shines like liquid gold.

In every corner of this earth,
We find anew our love's rebirth,
Unyielding as the mountain's crest,
Our bond remains, forever blessed.

As stars illuminate the skies,
We see our future in their eyes,
An untamed bond, so fierce, so true,
A love eternal, me and you.

Rogue Romance

We met beneath a moon so bright,
A rogue romance sparked in the night,
No rules, no bounds, our hearts so wild,
Two souls untamed, forever beguiled.

In secret gardens, shadows play,
We steal love's moments, night and day,
A whisper here, a stolen kiss,
In every touch, forbidden bliss.

Our paths converge in hidden ways,
Through tangled woods and misty rays,
A tale untold, yet boldly traced,
In every look, a love embraced.

No promises, just fleeting sighs,
Our rogue romance in disguise,
A dance beneath the canopy,
Of passion's deepest fantasy.

With hearts ablaze, we onward roam,
Through every storm, our love has grown,
A rogue romance, both fierce and free,
Two kindred spirits, you and me.

Eternal Frenzy

In shadows cast by moonlight's veil,
A mind entranced, a heart set sail,
Through endless nights and boundless dreams,
Where time dissolves in silken streams.

Whispers dance on midnight's breath,
A fevered pulse, a rhythm's death,
Desire's fire, an untamed blaze,
Lost in passion's wild maze.

Stars ignite in heaven's sweep,
Awakening secrets buried deep,
In frenzied tides of cosmic flow,
Boundless seas of fervent glow.

A lover's gaze, both fierce and tender,
Eternal bonds that none can sever,
In this dance of fate, entwined,
Hearts that race, forever blind.

Rogue Hearts

In twilight's hush, they find their place,
Two kindred souls in bold embrace,
Across the skies, a wild flight,
Through tempest's roar and darkest night.

With eyes that spark in cobalt blue,
Defying fate, they chase the new,
A rogue's path, untamed and free,
Their spirits wild, a boundless sea.

Through shadows thick, their love does glide,
No chains to bind, no rules abide,
In stolen moments, truth lays bare,
Rogue hearts that beat with daring flare.

A whispered vow, no need for words,
In silent strength, their song is heard,
A dance that only they can see,
In love, defiant, wild and free.

Boundless Yearning

In quiet depths of starlit night,
A hope ignites with gentle light,
A heart that whispers silent pleas,
For dreams that drift on cosmic seas.

Beneath the sky's eternal gaze,
A soul ensnared in yearning's blaze,
Time stands still, each breath a sigh,
In longing's tender, endless sky.

Through fields of dreams, a wanderer roves,
Boundless paths that love behoves,
A vision, sweet, so close yet far,
Like distant gleam of fading star.

In moments pure, a silent trust,
Desire's echo, more than lust,
A quest for more, in love's deep arc,
Boundless yearning, life's true mark.

Sensual Storm

Electric skies in tempest form,
Desires swirl in sensual storm,
Two bodies, close, a fevered dance,
In fervent waves, they take their chance.

Breathless whispers, urgent calls,
In passion's grasp, each barrier falls,
Their hearts collide, a rapturous quake,
In love's wild grip, they both awake.

Thunder rolls in echoed beat,
As souls in heated rhythm meet,
Each touch, a spark in night's cascade,
A storm of love, in shadows made.

In lightning's flash, their truth revealed,
Two hearts in storm forever sealed,
In passion's rain, they find their calm,
Sensual storm, a lover's psalm.

Rogue Kisses

Beneath the moon's soft, gentle gleam,
A stolen glance, an illicit dream,
Two souls collide in fate's wild chase,
In the shadows, they find their place.

Rogue kisses under night's dark veil,
Whisper secrets, begin the tale,
Silent promises in the hush,
Two hearts speed in a frenzied rush.

The stars look down, a silent choir,
Witness to a love set afire,
In stolen moments, passion's crest,
Boundless, endless, love professed.

Untamed Courtship

In fields of wild, where flowers bloom,
Two spirits dance, forego the gloom,
Their laughter rings through twilight skies,
A courtship free from rules and ties.

Hand in hand, they chase the wind,
Through life's wild maze, they'll never bend,
Eyes alight with untamed thrill,
Together, they surmount the hill.

In the wilderness, hearts are free,
Love's true form is plain to see,
An untamed courtship, bold and raw,
One that leaves the world in awe.

Reckless Hearts

Reckless hearts beat wild and free,
In the storm's embrace, their destiny,
A dance on edge, with no regard,
For caution is a distant bard.

Through tempest waves, in fierce delight,
They surge ahead, both day and night,
Twined in love's impetuous chase,
In every risk, they find their grace.

A love so bold, it conquers fear,
Through every storm, it draws them near,
Reckless hearts forever burn,
In each other's fire, they turn.

Untamed Serenade

A melody in the wild night air,
Soft whispers of a love laid bare,
An untamed serenade so pure,
With every note, their hearts allure.

Beneath the sky, a moonlit waltz,
Two souls in rhythm, without faults,
Their song echoes through the trees,
An ode to love, a sweet reprise.

In the night's embrace, they find,
A symphony that frees the mind,
An untamed serenade, it lingers long,
In their hearts, an endless song.

Ferocious Connection

Under a storm-battered sky, hands clasp tight,
In the distance, thunder roars its might.
Electric bolts trace our passionate align,
Ferocious tides in an ocean divine.

Eyes locked like prey and predator meet,
Heat smolders beneath our feet.
Unyielding hearts in wild, tempestuous flame,
Ferocious love with no need for name.

Words unsaid, a language of the beast,
Where silence feasts and chaos is released.
Soul ferocity dances in wickedly bright,
Connection forged in the heart of night.

Eternal roar within our veins pulses mad,
Combustion fierce in joy and sad.
Thunder and lightning mark our path,
Ferocious love, eternal and fast.

Echoes of passion in every touch,
In storms of love, there's never too much.
Raw and primal, our spirits are free,
Ferocious connection, wild as the sea.

Savanna Serenade

Whispers in the golden grass plains,
Beneath the sky where stillness reigns.
Harmony draped in warm embrace,
Savanna sings with tranquil grace.

Elephant's tread on earthen drum,
Rhythm of life where wild things come.
A lion's roar breaks morning mist,
Nature's orchestra cannot resist.

Acacias sway 'neath painted skies,
In dusky light where magic lies.
Zebras hum their striped allure,
Savanna's melody, wild and pure.

Heat shimmers rise in waves of song,
Antelopes leap, graceful and strong.
Birds compose a tune so grand,
Savanna serenade through the land.

Life's ancient music unfurls here,
In sounds so distant, yet so near.
Under the stars, dreamers parade,
Lost in the savanna serenade.

Wilderness of Us

We navigate the dense forest of being,
Branches of love, sharp and teeming.
In shadows cast, finding light,
Wilderness of us, deep in night.

Paths untamed and overgrown,
Together, yet sometimes alone.
A journey wild, with every breath,
Wilderness of us fights through death.

Rivers rush in untamed course,
Hearts entwined with nature's force.
Whispered secrets in moonlit trust,
Wilderness of us, love's robust.

Eyes like stars in twilight's haze,
Hands explore the endless maze.
Creatures call in voices grand,
Wilderness of us, hand in hand.

Mountains rise within our hearts,
No map can tear our souls apart.
Together through this wild expanse,
Wilderness of us, life's dance.

Free Spirits Entwined

Wind whispers through the open fields,
Free spirits embrace what love yields.
Hearts dance to a timeless beat,
Entwined in moments, wild yet sweet.

Laughter echoes in endless skies,
No boundaries where our freedom lies.
Grass beneath and stars above,
We roam the realms of infinite love.

Hand in hand, we chase the sun,
Every step, a journey begun.
No chains can bind our wanderlust,
Free spirits in the cosmic dust.

Breathing in the wild night's air,
Souls connected, pure and rare.
Through time and space, we are aligned,
Free spirits, eternally entwined.

Every dawn is a canvas blank,
Our love, the paint, along the bank.
Boundless, timeless, we are enshrined,
Free spirits forever entwined.

Savage Affection

In twilight's ruthless, tender embrace,
Whispers of love fill the space,
Wild as storms, gentle as the breeze,
Hearts intertwined in savage ease.

Eyes ablaze with untamed fire,
Yet touch as soft as silken attire,
Claws and comfort, both conspire,
To weave a bond that won't expire.

Tempests rage but calm ensues,
A dance of passion in varied hues,
Lovers' marks both sharp and kind,
Impressions left in body and mind.

Savage, yes, but oh so sweet,
Affection found in wild's heartbeat,
Where chaos meets serenity,
A love discovered in their unity.

The night may roar, the dawn may sigh,
But in those eyes, forever lies,
A savage love that won't diminish,
Endless, fierce, it has no finish.

Passion's Wilderness

Deep within the tangled wood,
Love ignites where shadows stood,
A forest wild with deep desire,
Burning bright with untamed fire.

Navigating paths unknown,
Hearts adventure, yet alone,
Through trials vast and meadows fair,
They find their solace hiding there.

Leaves of fervor, roots of lust,
In this wild, they place their trust,
Untamed spirits, free to roam,
Passion's wilderness, their home.

Unseen creatures whisper love,
Underneath the moon above,
Nature's symphony draws them near,
Every beat, a lover's cheer.

Leaves may fall and rivers dry,
But this wild spark will never die,
In passion's wild, they'll always find,
A haven sewn in heart and mind.

Ferocity of Desire

Eyes that pierce like midnight's spear,
A yearning that draws ever near,
Through the darkness, heat ignites,
Ferocity's flame in passion's rites.

Hungers deep that cease to rest,
Pulled by tides of burning zest,
Every touch, a spark, a blaze,
In this fervor, we are dazed.

Night unfolds in whispers raw,
Desires pressing, without a flaw,
A savage craving, wild, unchained,
In this fervor, sweetly pained.

Bound by lust yet feeling free,
Hearts embrace ferocity,
In love's fierce grip, they both confide,
Desire fierce, nowhere to hide.

When shadows flee and twilight breaks,
Their bond of flame unwavering takes,
A passion's beast, untamed, alive,
Ferocity in which they thrive.

Unleashed Emotions

Torrents surge within the heart,
An ocean wild, all torn apart,
Emotions bound, set loose again,
Echoes whisper through the rain.

Fierce and fleeting, soft yet strong,
In this storm, hearts belong,
Waves of passion, crest and break,
In their wake, unbound they ache.

No chains to hold, no ropes to bind,
A liberated, feral mind,
Love unleashed in untamed cries,
Underneath these open skies.

Raw and real, emotions flare,
In the tempest, they declare,
A truth that roars, unbridled, free,
In emotion's dance, they see.

When silence settles, calm imbues,
In the afterglow, they choose,
To live in freedom, love unlined,
Unleashed hearts forever twined.

Fierce Feelings

In the depths of hearts burning bright,
Passions flare in the darkest night.
Whispers turn to roaring flame
As fierce feelings ignite the same.

Eyes that pierce the soul's defense,
Words that cut with stark pretense.
In the dance of love's wild fire,
Every step brings hearts higher.

A storm brews within the touch,
Wrapping souls, but never too much.
Fierce feelings weave their tangled thread,
Binding spirits by paths they've shed.

With every pulse and ardent beat,
Love's fury refuses defeat.
Unyielding hearts in wild embrace,
Fierce feelings leave their trace.

Cascading Eros

Soft whispers on a moonlit shore,
A love that yearns, forevermore.
Cascading eros like rivers flow,
In tender moments, hearts bestow.

In every glance, a thousand dreams,
A love so pure, it deftly seems.
Those eyes speak words unspoken,
In their depth, a bond unbroken.

Gentle caress of time's sweet hand,
Two souls dance in love's command.
Cascading eros through endless night,
Love's tender touch, pure and bright.

Eros' arrow strikes so deep,
In memories, we'll always keep.
A love that flows, constant, free,
Cascading eros, you and me.

With every breath, we draw it near,
A love profound, forever dear.
Bound by fate, by stars alight,
Cascading eros in the night.

Tempestuous Union

In the eye of love's wild storm,
Two souls collide, their hearts transform.
Tempestuous winds weave them tight,
In the fury of a love so right.

Thunder rolls in whispered vows,
As lightning strikes with every rouse.
In the chaos of desire's flight,
Tempestuous union feels so light.

A dance of shadows, light entwine,
Bound together by love's design.
Tempest's edge, where passions soar,
Two hearts engaged forevermore.

Raindrops kiss in fierce embrace,
Each one a token of love's trace.
In the tempest, we're defined,
Tempestuous union, fate aligned.

Through the storm, our spirits fly,
In love's tempest, we defy.
Together, we weather night and day,
Tempestuous union, come what may.

Embers of Ardor

In the ashes of passion's blaze,
Embers glow, their tender praise.
Ardor's warmth in the silent night,
A love that lingers, burning bright.

Whispered tales by firelight,
In your arms, all feels right.
Embers of ardor softly gleam,
A love eternal, like a dream.

Gentle sparks that light our way,
In the heart, forever stay.
Through time's vast and endless sea,
Embers of ardor warm you and me.

As days fade into twilight's swell,
Our love's ember will always tell,
Of a flame that never dies,
In the embers, truth lies.

Holding close, our spirits tune,
Underneath the glowing moon.
In the dance of love's soft scar,
Embers of ardor guide afar.

Relentless Attraction

In silent rooms where shadows play,
A myriad dreams of you arise.
The night whispers your name in clay,
Underneath these starlit skies.

Your touch, a spark in darkness found,
Guides me through the winding mist.
Love's echo is a timeless sound,
In each and every tender twist.

Gravity cannot constrain,
This pull between our beating hearts.
Nothing is lost, nothing will wane,
As passion weaves its secret arts.

From dawn till dusk, in endless swirl,
My thoughts are threads entwined with yours.
Around your soul, my spirit twirls,
Forever seeking more and more.

No force on Earth could tear apart,
This relentless, strong attraction.
Bound together, mind and heart,
Lost in endless satisfaction.

Enthralled by Nature

Whispers of wind through towering trees,
Nature's song in every leaf.
In fields and forests, spirits please,
We find our solace, heal our grief.

Mountains rise, a silent chorus,
Each peak a story, ancient tale.
Valleys cradle, oceans implore us,
In their embrace, we never fail.

Rivers carve their endless quests,
Sparkling threads of liquid light.
Flowing hearts, in nature's breasts,
Find rest in whispers of the night.

Stars alight in midnight sky,
Constellations' gentle dance.
A cosmic spectacle lifts us high,
Within its cast, we take our chance.

Enthralled by nature's symphony,
We let our souls take flight.
In every hue and melody,
We find the essence of pure delight.

Uncaged Hearts

In gilded cages, locked and stored,
We left our dreams behind.
Wings clipped by chains we once adored,
Forbidden passions, undefined.

But time, relentless in its pace,
Unveils the hidden key.
Our hearts break free from their embrace,
To taste the air of liberty.

We soar beyond the gilded bars,
To realms where love is free.
In endless skies, beneath the stars,
We find our destiny.

Our hearts uncaged, they beat anew,
With every breath we take.
A love that's bold, a vow that's true,
In freedom's name, we awake.

Together now, in boundless flight,
No walls can hold us fast.
Uncaged hearts in the purest light,
Our love is made to last.

Nomadic Affection

Under skies of endless blue,
We wander, hand in hand.
Through lands where dreams are true,
Our spirits understand.

Each step a story left behind,
In sands of time and space.
Our love, a tether that we find,
In every fleeting place.

Mountains high and rivers wide,
Through deserts, forests green.
Together we, forever tied,
In moments still unseen.

No fixed abode, our hearts at play,
Across the world we roam.
Each dawn brings a new day,
In this, we make our home.

Affection's path is winding,
Yet constant in its course.
Our nomadic hearts are finding,
A love that's pure in force.

Unquenchable Desire

In the depths of night, I find your trace,
A longing touch, a warming embrace.
Whispered dreams, in shadows reside,
A quest for love, none can divide.

A spark ignites within my soul,
Unyielding flame I can't control.
Stars above paint tales untold,
Of passions burning bright and bold.

Through time and space, our spirits soar,
What we have, none will ignore.
A fervent wish, a lover's plea,
Boundless yearning sets us free.

In your eyes, I see our fate,
Infinite love, a timeless state.
Forever drawn, our hearts on fire,
A symphony of pure desire.

Unquenched thirst, unending need,
Love unchained shall always feed.
In your presence, life's complete,
Eternal bond, a love so sweet.

Mystic Enchantment

Under moonlit skies, a dance so rare,
Winds whisper secrets through the air.
Softly spoken spells take flight,
Enchanting hearts, embracing night.

Waves of magic weave their thread,
Dreams awakened, no fear to dread.
Mystic songs in twilight hum,
Inviting you to where I'm from.

Stars align to light our way,
In this realm where shadows play.
Mystic forces heed our call,
Lift our spirits, let them fall.

Veiled in mystery, pure delight,
Love's enchantment, soft and bright.
In every glance, in every sigh,
We trace our tales across the sky.

Sacred bond of endless lore,
Weaves a tapestry, forevermore.
Mystic paths our hearts align,
Love enchanted and divine.

Primitive Lust

In the wild where senses reign,
Raw desires break their chain.
Eyes that pierce through mortal veil,
Hunger burns, a feral tale.

Hands explore with savage might,
Fevered touch draws in the night.
Whispers fierce like flames of old,
Bodies meld in passion bold.

Jungle cries and nature's call,
Rhythms pound, let instincts thrall.
Primitive, untamed, and free,
Bound in pure ferocity.

Heartbeats drum like ancient sounds,
Lost in primal, sacred grounds.
Fusion of two souls on fire,
Yield to wild, untamed desire.

Limits fade, the world turns lush,
Inhibitions crushed to dust.
Embrace the wild, let it flow,
Primitive lust in every throe.

Irresistible Urge

Tangled thoughts of you and I,
Drawn like moths to flame on high.
Magnet force, unseen but strong,
Pulls our souls where we belong.

Across the room, your eyes invite,
A wordless song that feels so right.
Step by step, we close the gap,
Caught within this lover's trap.

Breathing deep, I sense your need,
A primal call, a lover's creed.
Skin to skin, the world fades out,
Lost in urge, beyond all doubt.

Silent whispers, gentle touch,
Kindling flames, it's all too much.
A yearning deep, we can't deny,
Vast and endless as the sky.

Irresistible urge that binds,
Woven threads of heart and mind.
In your hold, I find my place,
Timeless love, in sweet embrace.

Raw Tapestry

Threads of life weave through dreams,
In vibrant hues and silent streams,
Each moment, a delicate seam,
In the quilt of existence, it redeems.

Color spills on the canvas wide,
Stories told, in whispers they hide,
Bound by fate, yet world's collide,
In patterns eternal, we confide.

Fingers trace the woven line,
Searching for a hidden sign,
In the warp and weft, we find,
Truths that transcend space and time.

Crafted by hands both old and new,
Glimpses of light in every hue,
A tale of countless lives ensue,
In this fabric's endless view.

Embroidered fears, dreams foretold,
The tapestry's tale, brave and bold,
In every thread, a story sold,
Through nights of silver, days of gold.

Eruptive Embrace

Mountains tremble, skies ignite,
In a kiss of molten light,
Volcanic passion, pure delight,
In flames of rapture, we take flight.

Lava flows like liquid gold,
Tales of love, so fierce and bold,
In the heat, our souls unfold,
In an embrace, we fiercely hold.

Ash and soot, they intertwine,
In this dance, our hearts align,
Through the chaos, love divine,
In the blaze, eternities shine.

Nature's fury, gentle grace,
Found within your warm embrace,
A love that time cannot erase,
In the fire, we find our place.

From the depth of earth's desire,
Rises high, this burning pyre,
In the heart of passion's mire,
We ascend, lovers afire.

Barbaric Elegance

In wild hearts, a beauty lies,
Though fierce and raw, it never dies,
A dance beneath the savage skies,
In primal grace, the spirit flies.

Raging rivers carve their path,
Through storms and winds, nature's wrath,
Yet in chaos, art does hath,
A subtle, savage aftermath.

Untamed lands where eagles soar,
In every roar, a silent lore,
Though wild it seems, there's something more,
An elegance within the core.

Beauty found in untamed ways,
In the nights and in the days,
Barbaric elegance displays,
In primal, sacred, timeless praise.

Life's raw edge, a fierceness gleams,
Through jagged rocks and boundless streams,
A savage grace within our dreams,
In barbaric elegance, life redeems.

Passion's Untameability

In the heart, a wild flame,
Passion's call, it never tames,
Whispered words, unspoken names,
In the soul, it wildly claims.

Fires burn within our gaze,
In love's fierce, unyielding blaze,
Through the nights and endless days,
Untamed hearts set their ways.

Like the wind upon the sea,
Love's wild force, forever free,
In its grasp, we find the key,
A binding, untamed symphony.

Bound by neither chain nor tie,
In passion's realm, we choose to fly,
In this wild, uncharted sky,
Our souls ignite, soar high.

Unrestrained, our spirits flare,
In raw embrace, we lay bare,
Passion's untameability rare,
In love's wild breath, we share.

Volcanic Tenderness

Beneath the stone, within the core,
A molten heart begins to soar.
Silent whispers, warm embrace,
Unleashing fire, a gentle grace.

Lava flows, though tenderly,
A dance of flames, so wild and free.
Soft eruptions, passion's quest,
Within the earth, love manifests.

Heat and steam, with fervent touch,
Nature's ardor, felt so much.
Kindled by an inner spark,
Illuminates the deepest dark.

Molten rivers, veins of light,
Blazing trails through endless night.
In the quiet, sparks do sing,
Tender heart of a volcanic king.

Gentle burns, yet fiercely kind,
A love like this, so hard to find.
Underneath the rugged crust,
Lies a tender, loving trust.

Heart of the Wild

In the forest, shadows play,
Where wild creatures softly stray.
Whispers carry on the breeze,
Tales untamed among the trees.

Beasts and birds, a symphony,
Nature's wild, an untamed sea.
Hearts that beat with primal call,
Free and fierce, despite it all.

Leaves that rustle, wild and free,
Branches swaying, wild decree.
Life explodes in emerald hues,
Heart of wild, life renews.

Echoes deep in lunar light,
Wild heartbeats, a silent rite.
In the night, the world aligns,
Untamed hearts and wild pines.

Mystic paths through wooded lands,
Guided by unseen hands.
Heart of wild, untamed and true,
Nature's love, forever new.

Rebel Heartbeats

Echoes from a distant cry,
Hearts that dare to reach the sky.
Breaking chains, free will's decree,
Breathing wild, forever free.

Bound by neither rule nor fear,
Living lives intense and clear.
Rush of pulse, a rebel's song,
Fight for right, defy the wrong.

Beats that surge beneath the skin,
Rebel hearts, they rise within.
Rhythm strong, electric fire,
Dance to dreams of fierce desire.

Waves of courage, bold and bright,
In the dark, they bring the light.
Unyielding in the face of strife,
Rebels live a fiery life.

Heartbeats loud, in proud defiance,
Freedom's breath, in bold alliance.
With each pulse, a promise sworn,
Rebel hearts are never torn.

Untamed Hearts

In the quiet of the night,
Untamed hearts bathe in moonlight.
Freedom whispers through the dark,
Kindling love's unbound spark.

Wander far, the world to see,
Untamed hearts, wild and free.
Paths unknown and skies untried,
Together, life a daring ride.

Hands that hold, but never chain,
Love that falls like gentle rain.
Boundless skies and endless dreams,
Hearts united in moonbeams.

No constraints can limit flight,
In the wild, they find their right.
Harmony in wildest form,
Souls connected, brightly warm.

Adventures call, they heed the quest,
Untamed love, they are blessed.
In each other, they find peace,
Untamed hearts, their love's release.

Erotic Frenzy

In shadows deep where secrets lie,
Our bodies speak without a sigh.
Hands that trace, desires unbind,
In a dance where souls entwine.

Senses flare, a burning fire,
Every touch, an artful lyre.
Hearts that race with fevered beat,
As we fall, our worlds complete.

Lips that whisper sin's delight,
In the dark, no wrong, no right.
Bound by passion's endless maze,
In this lust, we lose our days.

Breathless sighs and fervent pleas,
Lost in waves of ecstasy.
No escape from this embrace,
In this frenzy, time and space.

Night crescendoes with our cries,
Underneath the midnight skies.
Erotic dreams, our hearts afire,
Consumed by this torrid desire.

Savage Serenade

Winds that howl through forests deep,
Where wild things in secrets keep.
Echoes of a savage song,
Where nature's chorus does belong.

Mountains high and rivers wide,
Underneath a starry tide.
Wolves that call the night their own,
Untamed hearts, to wilderness they are shown.

In the glade where shadows dance,
Eyes that pierce with savage glance.
Untamed beauty, fierce and wild,
Nature's pure, untarnished child.

Roaring fires under the moon,
From the dark, the owl's tune.
A serenade so wild, so free,
The forest sings its symphony.

Between the trees, the spirits play,
In the night, they find their way.
A savage serenade so true,
In nature's arms, we are renewed.

Unfettered Longing

Stars that glisten in the night,
Holding dreams within their light.
An unfettered longing stirs,
In whispers of lost demurs.

Eyes that seek across the void,
Yearning hearts that can't avoid.
Love that travels time's expanse,
In a never-ending dance.

Chasing shadows, chasing dreams,
Nothing's ever as it seems.
Souls that wander, never rest,
In their quest, they are blessed.

Through the silence, longing speaks,
In the moments, solace seeks.
Yet this longing won't subside,
For it's love that we confide.

Endless nights and boundless days,
Unfettered longing always stays.
In this ache, we find our song,
Love, the journey all along.

Untamed Bliss

Whispers of a breeze so light,
Underneath the cloak of night.
Hearts that beat with wild grace,
In a lost, enchanted place.

Eyes that dance with fervent gleam,
In the midst of silent dream.
Hands that reach, but never bind,
In this bliss, they're intertwined.

Laughter echoes in the air,
Untamed joy without a care.
Bound by nothing but the stars,
As we break through all our bars.

In the wild where silence sings,
Freedom's pure, unbridled wings.
Bliss that knows no chains, no bounds,
In the soul, its song resounds.

Boundless skies and endless seas,
In this bliss, our hearts are free.
Untamed, wild, forevermore,
In this joy, our spirits soar.

Untamed Hearts

In the forest where the shadows dance,
Two hearts beat wild in sweet romance.
Unafraid of nature's dark embrace,
Together they find their sacred place.

Emotions run like rivers deep,
In moonlit nights they silently weep.
Bound not by chains, nor time's cruel art,
They share the rhythm of each heart.

Through tempest winds and skies so gray,
Their love persists come night or day.
Earth's untamed beauty mirrors their flame,
A love unbroken, wild, untamed.

Barefoot they walk on paths unknown,
Their spirits rise, no longer alone.
Roots entwined, and branches free,
They carve their love in every tree.

Stars bear witness from high above,
To this raw, untamed kind of love.
No force on earth can tear apart,
These fierce, unbridled, untamed hearts.

Feral Embrace

In twilight's veil, they find their grace,
Two souls entwined in a feral embrace.
With whispers soft like autumn leaves,
They cherish secrets the forest weaves.

Eyes that glint with wild desire,
Hearts that blaze with untamed fire.
In nature's arms, they find their place,
Locked forever in a feral embrace.

Beneath the canopy of ancient trees,
Their spirits dance with every breeze.
A feral bond, no time can erase,
In endless fervor, they embrace.

Moonlight bathes the lovers' trail,
Guiding them through the mystic veil.
In twilight's glow, they set their pace,
Forever bound in a feral embrace.

With every touch, their wildness grows,
Among the ferns where freedom flows.
In nature's arms, they find solace,
Locked forever in a feral embrace.

Passionate Wilderness

A realm where wildflowers bloom,
Hearts beat in the forest's womb.
Underneath the starlit skies,
Their love's a fire that never dies.

In the whispering pines they stray,
Through the moss and fern they play.
No boundaries can hold them back,
Their love's a never-ending track.

Eyes meet in the dawn's first light,
In the passionate wilderness of night.
Each touch ignites their hearts afresh,
In nature's arms, they intermesh.

With every step, their spirits rise,
In synch with earth and open skies.
Unbound by rules, unfazed by time,
Their hearts create a perfect rhyme.

In this wild land where freedom rings,
Their souls take flight on untamed wings.
In the passionate wilderness divine,
Their love stands the test of time.

Savage Devotion

In the dark where wild things grow,
Two hearts find a savage flow.
Untamed love, fierce and bold,
Their story in whispers told.

Through the storm and raging fire,
They chase their every heart's desire.
Unfettered by the world's decree,
Their savage love forever free.

Barefoot on the path unseen,
Their love remains forever keen.
In nature's hold, they fight and kiss,
A union of feral bliss.

Eyes that burn with ancient might,
Hearts aglow in the pale moonlight.
Yet in the chaos, they find devotion,
Tied forever by wild emotion.

Roots entwined beneath their feet,
In every heartbeat, a fierce beat.
In the wild, their love is shown,
Savage devotion all their own.

Innate Yearning

In the depths of silent night,
Whispers soft, a soul's delight,
Dreams cascade in silver streams,
Bathing hearts in moonlit beams.

Stars above like augured fates,
Guide the lover to the gates,
Where desire and passion blend,
In a song that knows no end.

Silent winds may carry sighs,
Born from love, the heart complies,
Longing pulses through the air,
Stirring whispers everywhere.

Endless search for the divine,
In the eyes where lover's shine,
Binds us in this eternal quest,
Where our spirits find their rest.

Underneath the twilight skies,
Promises in lover's eyes,
Yearn for moments yet untold,
In their arms, they break the mold.

Unchained Cravings

Cravings dance in fire's embrace,
Hungry hearts, a ruthless chase,
In the shadows, secrets bare,
Passion blooms in midnight's air.

Words unspoken, bodies drawn,
To the rhythm, to the dawn,
Unchained cravings, wild and free,
Lost in waves of ecstasy.

Through the night, the flames ignite,
Burning fierce with pure delight,
Passions roar as hearts conspire,
Fanned by winds of wild desire.

In the silence, breathing deep,
Cravings potent as they seep,
Through the night and into day,
Wild hearts in fervor play.

Chains of longing, broken wide,
Unleashed hunger side by side,
Cravings sing in vibrant tones,
Hearts unchained find their home.

Primeval Romance

In forests deep, where shadows speak,
Tales of love that eons seek,
Primeval whispers, ancient lore,
Echoes ring from times of yore.

Beneath the boughs of trees so grand,
Lovers walk through twilight's sand,
Fingers lace and hearts entwine,
In romantic, ancient rhyme.

Moonlight bathes the forest floor,
Illuminates what hearts adore,
Timeless dance of love's embrace,
Marked by nature's silent grace.

Stars align in cosmic drift,
Lovers' spirits prone to lift,
Whispers float on evening tide,
Bound by love, they gently glide.

Primeval romance, wild and pure,
Strength in love does reassure,
Eons pass but hearts remain,
A dance eternal, never wane.

Lustful Dominion

Eyes that pierce through velvet night,
Claim the soul in pure delight,
In lustful dominion, hearts collide,
Where shadows deep and secrets hide.

Torch of passion fiercely burns,
In its glow, desire churns,
Dominion taken, love unbound,
In the silence, hearts resound.

Hands explore with fervent quest,
Seeking more, they find no rest,
Dominion's rule, by lust defined,
Crossing thresholds, hearts combined.

In the whispers of the dark,
Echoes of love, a vital spark,
Dominion craves, forevermore,
Lustful reign at passion's core.

Bound by fervor, hearts enflamed,
In dominion, love unclaimed,
Rule of lust, they both abide,
In this realm where love resides.

Untamed Flames

In the heart where fires birth
Burns the spirit, unbridled, free.
Every ember, a vow of worth,
   Dances wild upon the sea.

Whispers crackle in the night,
   Echoes of a passion pure,
Blazing trails beyond the sight,
   Of spirits bold and sure.

Silhouettes against the dark,
   A shadowplay of dreams,
Every spark, a life ignites,
In the moon's ethereal beams.

Fury fierce, yet tender sweet,
   Winds of change, they roar,
Hearts converge where fires meet,
And love's wild flames explore.

Unchained, the fire's rhythm sways,
   In a dance of timeless art,
Glimmering in twilight's haze,
Living embers of the heart.

Raw Infatuation

Eyes that lock in silent pledge,
Whispers neither dare to share,
A dance along the passion's edge,
Breath caught in the midnight air.

Hands that tremble, almost touch,
Eager, yet restrained, they stay,
Yearning hearts that throb too much,
In the heat of the unspoken fray.

Every glance, a secret told,
Between souls too young to claim,
A fevered dream, both hot and cold,
In the throes of infatuation's flame.

Lips that hover, just in reach,
Promises in silence swore,
Raw enchantment's fervent speech,
Between hearts that ache for more.

Love, unpolished, boldly true,
In its raw, untamed delight,
In a garden where passions grew,
And hearts take flight into the night.

Boundless Ardor

Where the sky meets endless sea,
Hearts converge in boundless grace,
Waves of passion, wild and free,
In an eternal, sweet embrace.

Eyes that find the soul's true core,
Silent vows in twilight made,
Every moment held in store,
Where love's infinite cascade.

Hands entwined in fervent clasp,
Hearts illuminate the night,
Whispers in the stars, we grasp,
A bond that outshines all light.

Kisses crowned by moonbeams' glow,
Nurtured by the warmth within,
Every beat and breath below,
A testament to where love's been.

Endless as the cosmic tide,
Ardor bound by naught but dream,
Souls in unison, they stride,
Through life's boundless ardor's theme.

Untapped Euphoria

Beneath the skies, so wide and blue,
Lies a joy yet unexplored,
In moments tender, precious, few,
A euphoric feeling stored.

Hearts that leap in newfound cheer,
With laughter pure and wild,
Chasing dreams without a fear,
In the spirit of a child.

Eyes that see the world anew,
Every color, bright and clear,
In every drop of morning dew,
Echoes of a joy sincere.

Embrace the thrill of unknown lands,
Untapped moments pure and bright,
In every touch of holding hands,
Thrives a euphoric rite.

Life's uncharted, joyous wave,
Flows where dreams and passions meet,
In untapped euphoria, we brave,
Every moment, soft and sweet.

Furious Affection

In turmoil's grasp, a love aflame,
Passions mix in tender blame,
Hearts collide in a fierce embrace,
Echoes of anger, yet full of grace.

Eyes alight with fervent fire,
Moments ripple with desire,
Words that cut and then repair,
Unyielding bond beyond compare.

When storm subsides, all's tender still,
A softened glance, a gentle thrill,
Despite the rage, beneath the strife,
Furious affection breathes life.

Hands that argue, hands that mend,
Two destinies forever blend,
In love's fierce cycle, find their way,
A tumultuous but enduring stay.

No sorrow lingers, only light,
In the shadows of the night,
Furious affection, bold and bright,
Holds us close and makes things right.

Nocturnal Desires

Under the moon's soft silver gleam,
Whispers dance in twilight's dream,
Touch of shadows, a lover's call,
Nighttime's veil does softly fall.

In the quiet, hearts awaken,
By the moon's allure, we're taken,
A silent wish, a midnight kiss,
Nocturnal desires, endless bliss.

Stars above, in lustrous glow,
Guide us to where passions flow,
In the darkness, bold and free,
Nocturnal desires come to be.

Through darkness deep, we navigate,
In the stillness, hearts relate,
Secret whispers, hidden fires,
Fueling midnight's deep desires.

When dawn approaches with her light,
We're left to long for each night,
Until the moon does rise once more,
Nocturnal desires to explore.

Savage Symphony

In the wild, the music calls,
Nature's notes, like thunder falls,
Roaring rivers, winds that play,
Savage symphony guides the way.

Beasts and birds, together sing,
Echoes through the forest ring,
In chaos pure, a primal tie,
Underneath the open sky.

Mountains high and valleys deep,
Songs of the wild, ancient, steep,
Beating hearts in wild display,
Savage symphony holds sway.

From dawn till dusk, the concert runs,
Through moonlit fields, past setting suns,
Each note a cry, a call, a plea,
In nature's savage symphony.

Untamed power in every chord,
Spells of wonder are outpoured,
Living, breathing, wild and free,
Life's own savage symphony.

Unpredictable Passion

In chances taken, hearts unfold,
With stories yet to be told,
Unseen paths, an unknown flight,
Passion's spark ignites the night.

Eyes meet eyes, the world stands still,
Unpredictable and thrilling thrill,
In chaos, find the heart's true beat,
A burning flame, a wild heat.

Moments fleeting, desires strong,
In each other's arms, where we belong,
Unexpected twists, an open door,
Unpredictable passion forevermore.

Risk and wonder, hand in hand,
Upon this fervent, shifting sand,
Love's an adventure, bold yet sweet,
Unpredictable passion at our feet.

With each turn, a new surprise,
In tangled destiny's eyes,
Waltzing through uncertainty,
Unpredictable passion, wild and free.